Celebration!
The Millennium and Beyond

by Jan Holdstock
edited by Alison Hedger

Suitable for Key Stages 2+3

A celebration in music and presentation
for use prior to and into the New Millennium

There are five sections, each with a song and spoken presentation.
The length of this work depends upon how it is performed,
but it will be from 15 minutes upwards if all five songs are sung.

SECTIONS

1. Keeping Time
2. Time's Too Short
3. Twenty-First Century Children
4. Singing And Dancing
5. Celebration

SONGS

1. Time Passes	*Three parts + optional recorder*	
2. We Didn't Have Time	*Two parts + optional recorder for Refrain*	
3. 21st Century Children	*Unison + optional recorder*	
4 Singing A Song Together	*Unison + recorder, percussion, clapping and movement*	
5. Celebration!	*Three parts + recorder and bells*	

A matching tape cassette of the music for rehearsals and performances is available,
Order No. GA11065, side A with vocals included and side B with vocals omitted.

Pupil's Book Order No. GA11064 contains the linking sections, song words and choir and recorder parts.

© Copyright 1998 Golden Apple Productions
A division of Chester Music Limited
8/9 Frith Street, London W1V 5TZ
Teacher's Book Order No. GA11063

ISBN 0-7119-6827-6

Welcome to another Jan Holdstock Golden Apple publication: **Celebration! The Millennium and Beyond**. This is a versatile work which gives teachers a framework upon which they can build. The work is divided into five sections, and each section is given a title. It is possible to develop the sections further through topic work. Some suggestions are given below, but these ideas are not exhaustive. Please make as much, or as little of the linking sections as is appropriate to your needs. Alternatively, you may wish to dispense with the linking sections altogether, and just use some or all of the songs.

The recorder parts are indicated as optional in places. This means that nothing will be lost musically should you not include the recorders, but the parts are there giving you the option to use them as needs arise. Please feel free to arrange the music for any available instruments. This is a celebration, and a good time to include as many participants as possible.

By the way, some people think that the New Millennium and the 21st Century will be celebrated in the year 2001. Perhaps you may choose to have your celebration then. Some alternative words have been provided for use after the year 2000, making Jan Holdstock's clever songs suitable both for the run up to the New Millennium and on, well into the next century. So whatever your views on the Millennium, Golden Apple wishes you the happiest of celebrations.

Alison Hedger

SECTIONS	**POSSIBLE TOPIC LINKS**
1. Keeping Time	Science, Maths, History, Technology
2. Time's Too Short	Religious Instruction
3. Twenty First Century Children	History
4. Singing and Dancing	Performing Arts and Geography
5. Celebration!	History

1 TIME PASSES

Three parts + optional recorder

Positively ♩ = 130

All: 1. How do we know the time is pass-ing?__ There are so
ma - ny ways._ Each day rolls on in-to night - time. Each night rolls

1st Refrain

back to day.___ Six - ty min - utes in an hour.

Twen - ty - four hours a day. Three hun - dred and six - ty - five

days in a year.___ Time pas - ses on its way.

Recorder

All: 2. How do we know the time is pass-ing?__ The sea-sons come and go.__

We watch our friends grow-ing old - er, and we grow old - er too.__ *div.*

2nd Refrain

Part 1

Six - ty min - utes in an hour. Twen - ty-four hours a day. Three

Part 2

Tick - tock, tick - tock, tick - tock, tick - tick - a - tick - tock.

sim.

6

hun-dred and six - ty-five days in a year._ Time pas - ses on its way.

Tick - tock, tick - tock, tick - tock, tick.

Recorder

3. Some - times we show that time is pass - ing._ We wel - come each new year._

Part 1

Part 2

Tick - tock, tick - tock, tick - tock, tick - tick - a - tick - tock.

Coda

2 WE DIDN'T HAVE TIME

Two parts + optional recorder for the Refrain

Gently ♩. = 70

It's two

Refrain

Recorder

thou - sand years since Je - sus was born with man - y things done in His

name.___ But is the world___ ve - ry diff - 'rent to - day, or are we___ just the

*could also be played by recorder

3 21ST CENTURY CHILDREN

Unison + optional recorder

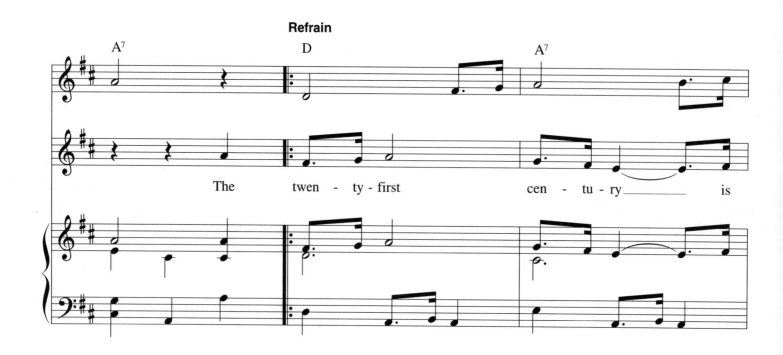

The twen - ty - first cen - tu - ry_____ is

going to be the time we know. The twen - ty - first

cen - tu - ry, _____ a time for us to live and grow. We've got

twen - ti - eth cen - tu - ry Mums and Dads, Gran - nies and Grand - dads

too. But we're going to live in a cen-tu-ry that's

to finish

new, brand new.

rit.

to continue

new, brand new.
1. As we meet our
2. As we use our

14

cen - tu - ry, let us greet each pass - ing day. Let us
cen - tu - ry, don't a - buse the world we share. Spread the

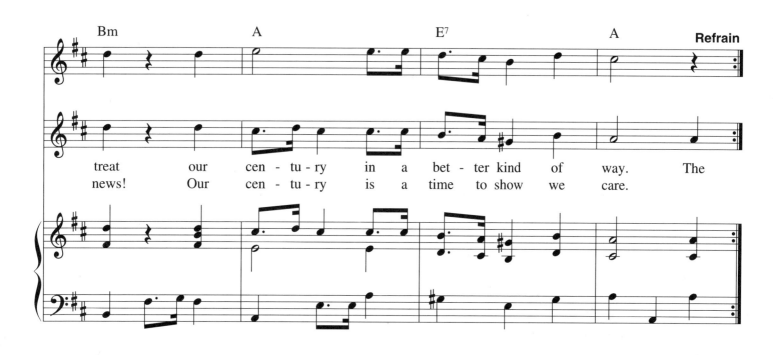

treat our cen - tu - ry in a bet - ter kind of way. The
news! Our cen - tu - ry is a time to show we care.

4 SINGING A SONG TOGETHER

Unison + recorder, percussion, clapping and movement

With a happy bounce – a community song feel ♩ = 120

1. Ever - y - bod - y loves sing - ing. It
2. Ever - y - bod - y loves danc - ing. And
*3. (see note below)

start - ed long a - go. When peo - ple were hap - py or
soon the time will come. For - get all your trou - bles and

* Verse 3. Music repeats and children play percussion instruments, dance and move as appropriate.
The REFRAIN is sung.

when they were sad, they had to let their feel - ings____ show.
move to the beat.____ We wel-come(d) the Mil - len - ni - um.

Refrain

Sing - ing a song____ to - geth - er, danc - ing to the mus - ic's____

beat. It does - n't mat - ter____ where you are,

in the coun - try or a ci - ty____ street.____ Peo - ple from ev - er - y

nat - ion, peo - ple old and__ young,

join the cel - e - bra - tion when a song is sung.

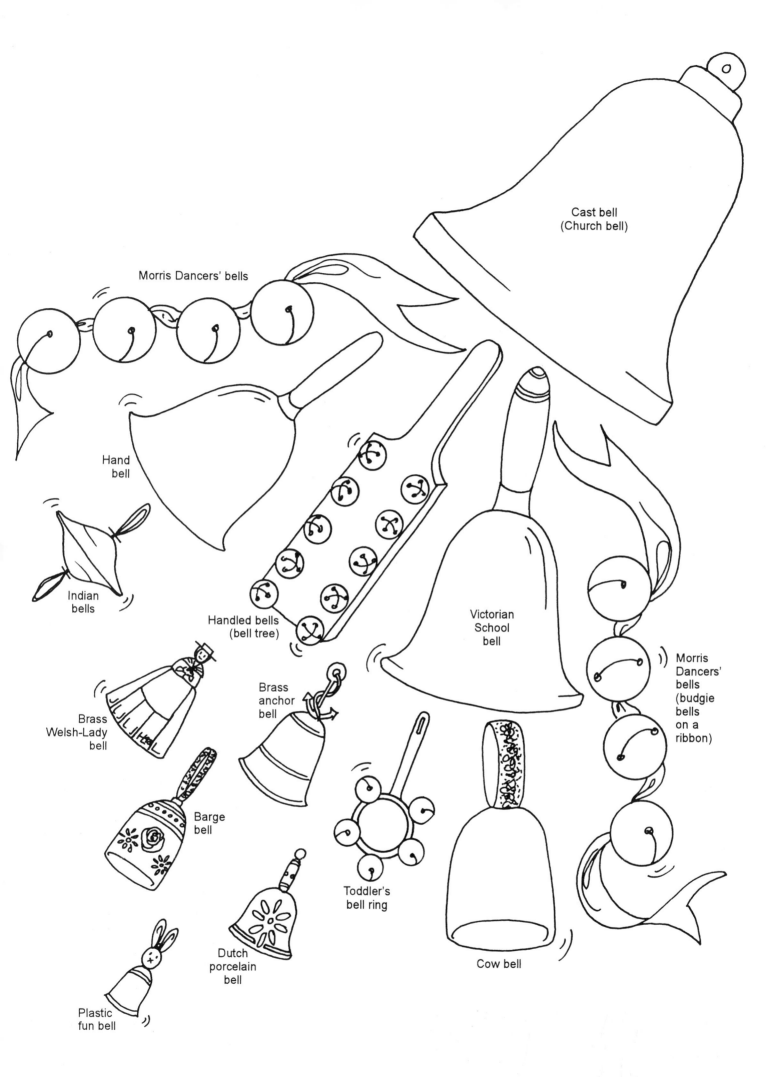

Cast bell
(Church bell)

Morris Dancers' bells

Hand
bell

Indian
bells

Handled bells
(bell tree)

Victorian
School
bell

Morris
Dancers'
bells
(budgie
bells
on a
ribbon)

Brass
Welsh-Lady
bell

Brass
anchor
bell

Barge
bell

Toddler's
bell ring

Dutch
porcelain
bell

Plastic
fun bell

Cow bell

5 CELEBRATION!

Three parts + recorder and bells

Verses 1, 2 and 3 are firstly sung in unison by everyone. Then there is an instrumental linking section of recorder and piano. This is followed by the simultaneous singing of the three verses through twice, with the recorder also playing.

Alternative words to Song 5 for use after the Millennium

1. *Another year has come and gone,*
   The bells have celebrated with each ring.
   And now we'll give a cheer
   For another year.
   Days of trust and hope appear.

2. *Ring out with gladness, all bells.*
   Ring them out from every steeple.
   Ring out, the New Year is here.
   Celebrate, ye people.

3. *Ding dong, ding dong,*
   Ding dong, ding-a-dong-a-ding dong.
   Ding dong, ding dong,
   Ding dong, ding.

9/99 (35216)

Also by Jan Holdstock
for Key Stages 2 and 3

A Christmas Welcome

Jan Holdstock

The Christmas Nativity story retold through narration and seven attractive songs for junior choirs, Church groups and all those who love to sing. The songs can be sung alone or performed together as a cantata. Alternatively, mime or a play can be added to create a Nativity.

Teacher's book GA11028
Pupil's book GA11029
Matching tape cassette GA11030

In Viking Times

Jan Holdstock

Ideal for cross-curricular Key Stage 2 Viking projects: an all-year-round musical presentation with six songs in unison, two and three parts plus narration. Illustrations of Viking characters are included which will stimulate costume ideas and the teacher's book contains useful 'Did You Know' facts.

Teacher's book GA11035
Pupil's book GA11036
Matching tape cassette GA11037

Footprints on the Moon
Apollo 11

Jan Holdstock

The true story of the first landing on the moon retold in narration and five new songs, plus recorder parts. Can be performed as a concert piece or used as a musical framework for a historical space drama.

Teacher's book GA11053
Pupil's book GA11054
Matching tape cassette GA11055

GOLDEN APPLE PRODUCTIONS
A division of Chester Music Limited
Exclusive distributors:
Music Sales Limited, Newmarket Road, Bury St Edmunds, Suffolk IP33 3YB

More best-selling authors from Golden Apple...

A Victorian Christmas Party

Key Stage 2

Music by Alison Hedger Words by Sheila Wainwright

A brilliant cross-curricular musical ideal for topic work, combining all the fun of a traditional Christmas party with a look at the Victorian period – upstairs and downstairs. Includes nine sparkling new songs, a Nativity tableau and lots of opportunities for dance and humorous interpretation. Alison Hedger has written many well-known and loved Christmas Nativities and shows for children.

Teacher's book GA11056
Pupil's play book GA11058
Matching tape cassette GA11057

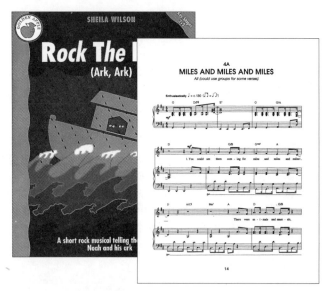

Rock The Boat!

Key Stages 2 and 3

Sheila Wilson

A short, upbeat rock musical telling the story of Noah and his ark. Five great songs with witty lyrics in a variety of styles and lively rhyming narrative. A bit of sadness and a lot of fun – another unmissable musical in Sheila Wilson's popular and distinctive style!

Teacher's book GA11047
Pupil's word book GA11048
Matching tape cassette GA11049

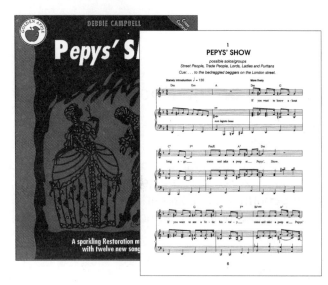

Pepys' Show

Key Stages 2 and 3

Debbie Campbell

A fine Restoration musical with twelve lively new songs taking us back in history and recalling with humour the Restoration of Charles II, the Bubonic Plague and the Great Fire of London. A superb way to bring history alive for children, complemented by Debbie Campbell's entertaining and attractive music.

Teacher's book GA11050
Pupil's book GA11051
Matching tape cassette GA11052

A catalogue of the complete range of Golden Apple children's educational music, from pre-school to Key Stage 3, is available on request.

GOLDEN APPLE PRODUCTIONS
A division of Chester Music Limited
Exclusive distributors:
Music Sales Limited, Newmarket Road, Bury St Edmunds, Suffolk IP33 3YB